The Wobbly Stick Man

For artists ready to move on
from drawing stick figures

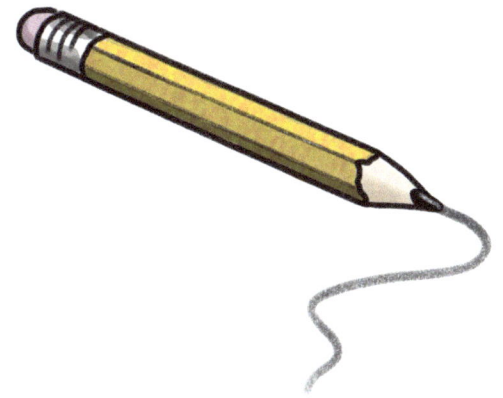

Saul was the luckiest stick man in the world.

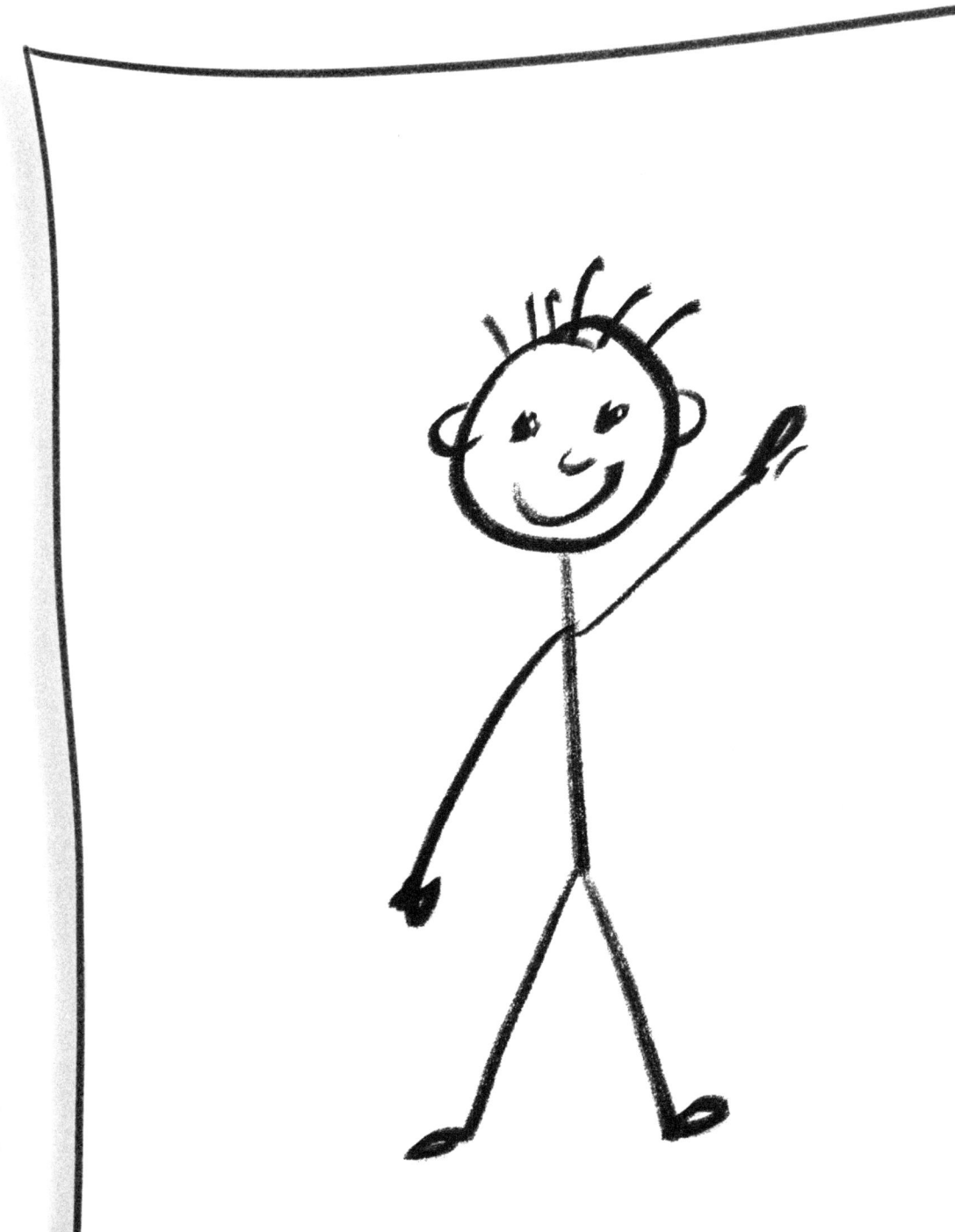

Today he got his wish!

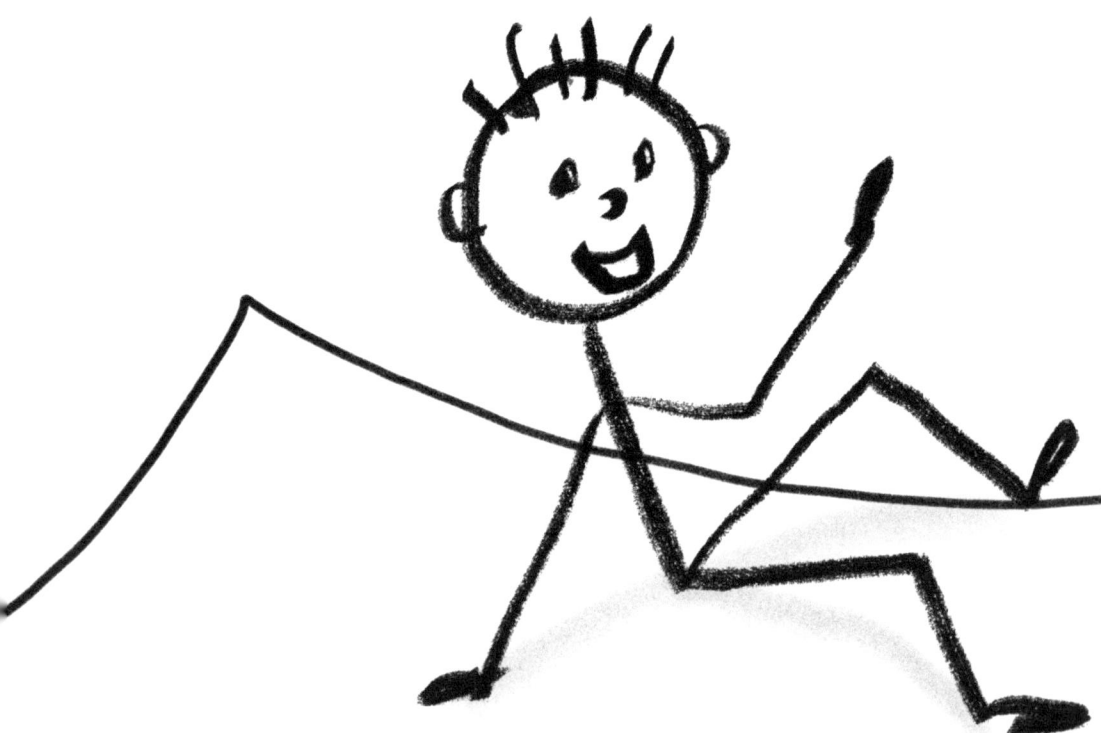

He got to leave the paper he was drawn on and come to life!

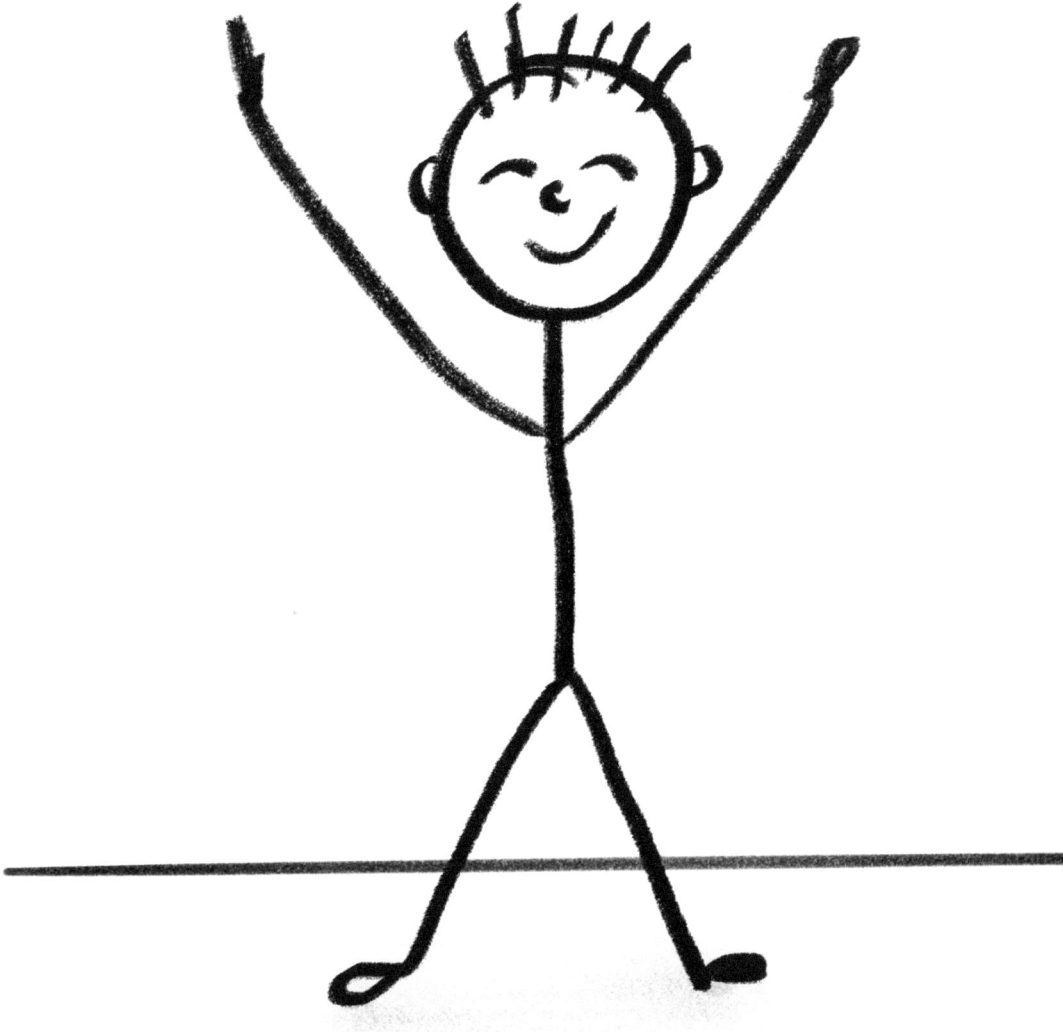

Suddenly, Saul started to wobble,

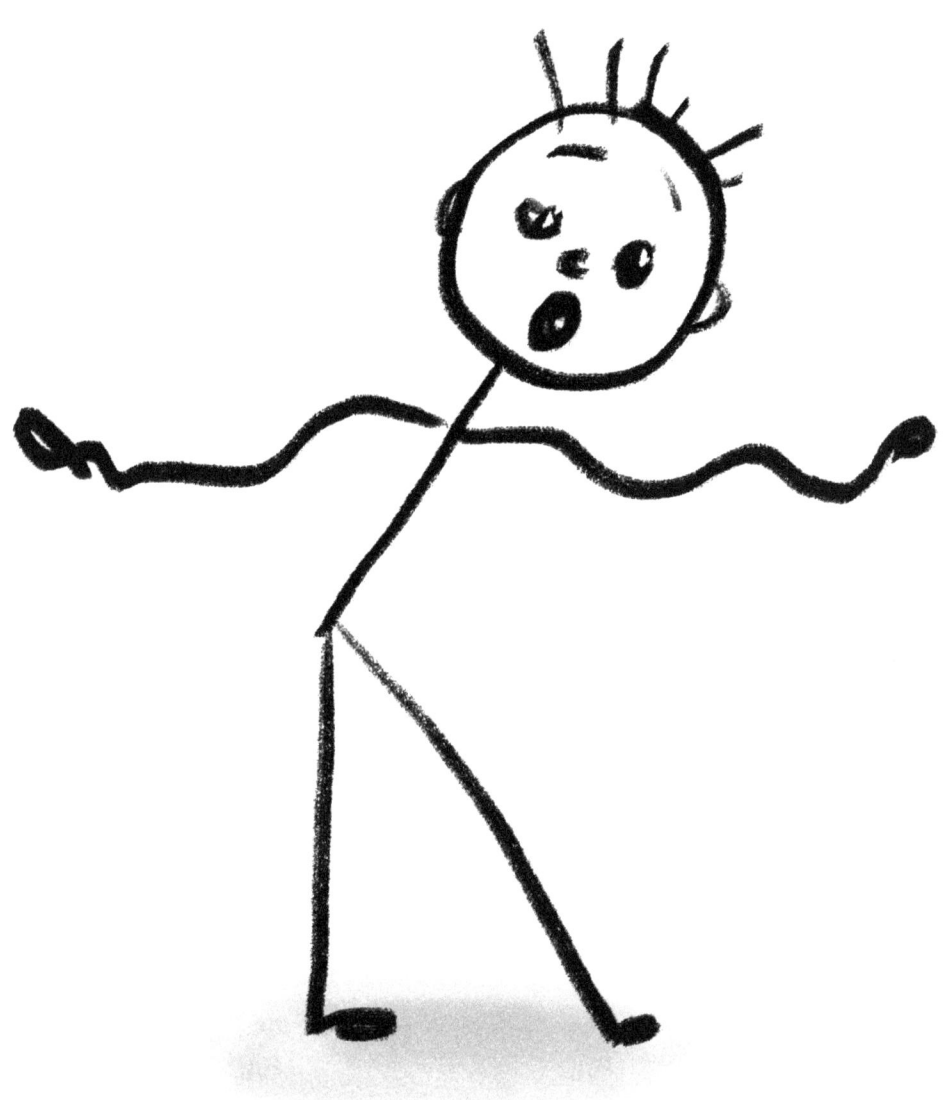

and his heavy head fell to the ground with a *thump!*

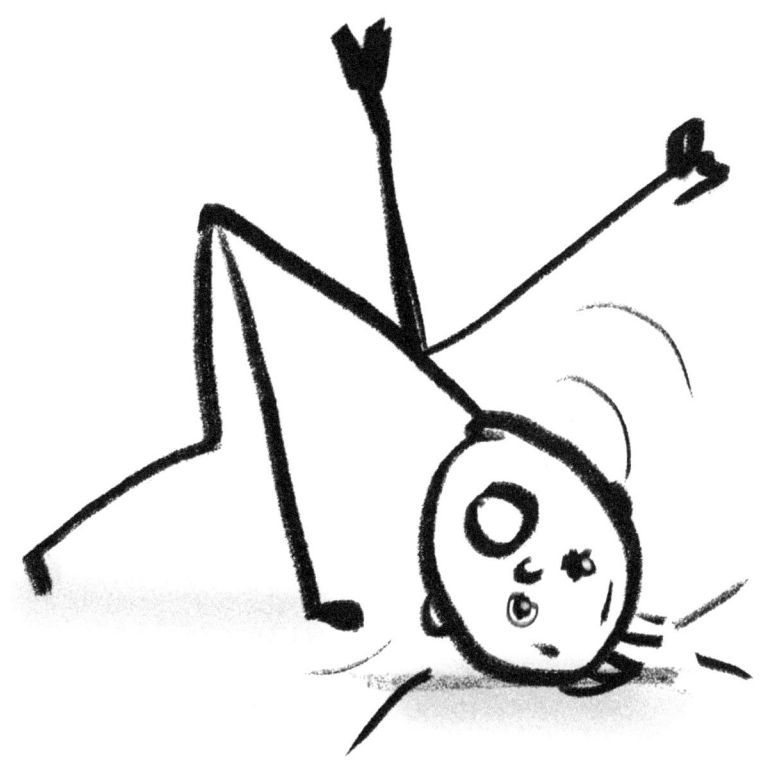

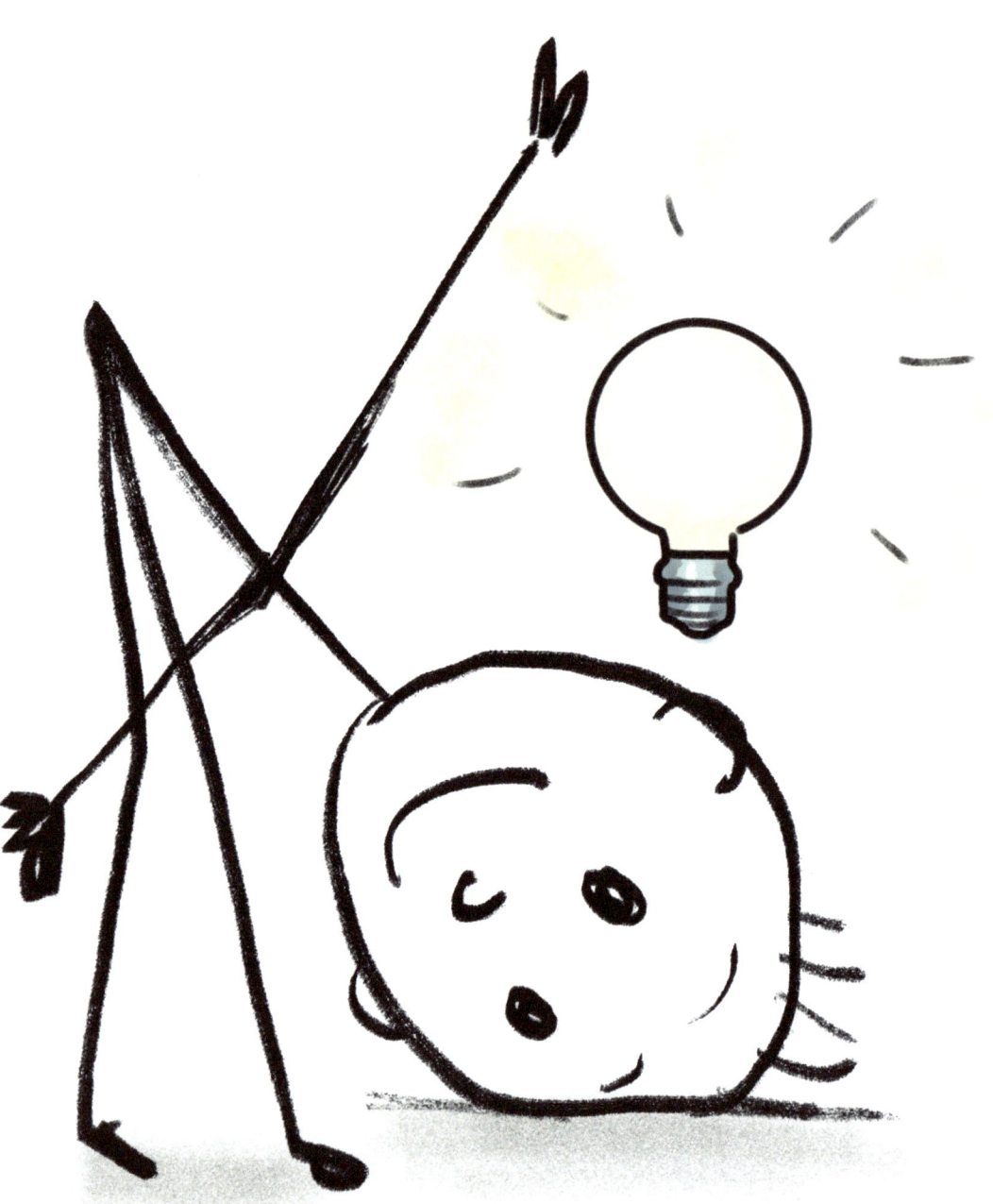

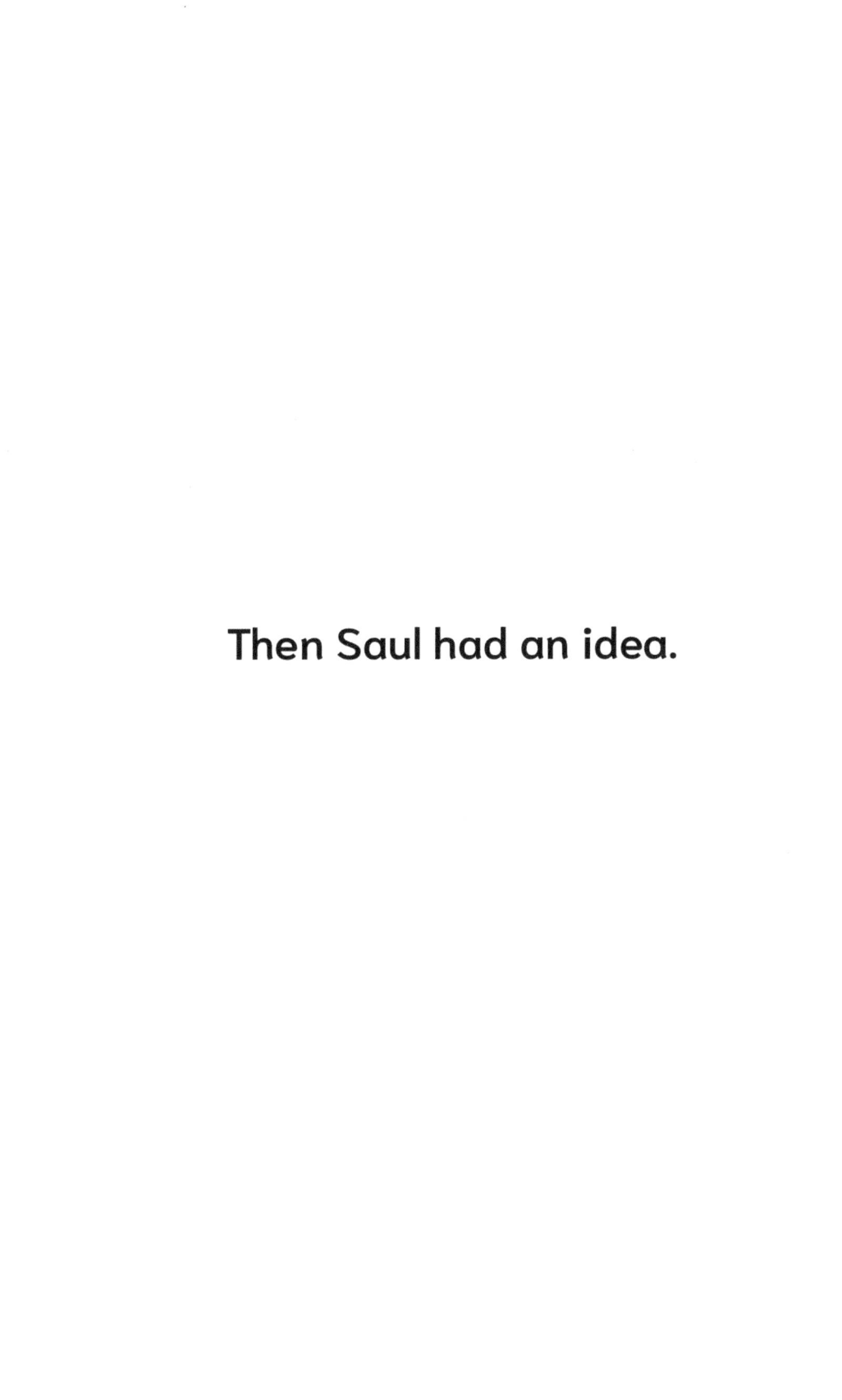

Then Saul had an idea.

Saul needed a body to support the weight of his head. He grabbed a pencil and drew a nice, sturdy rectangle.

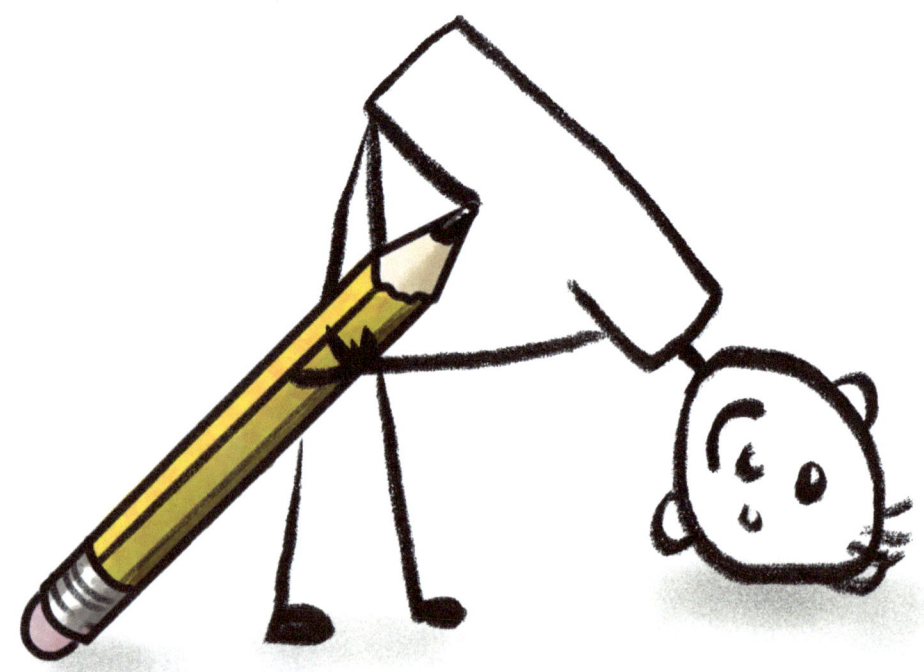

Success!

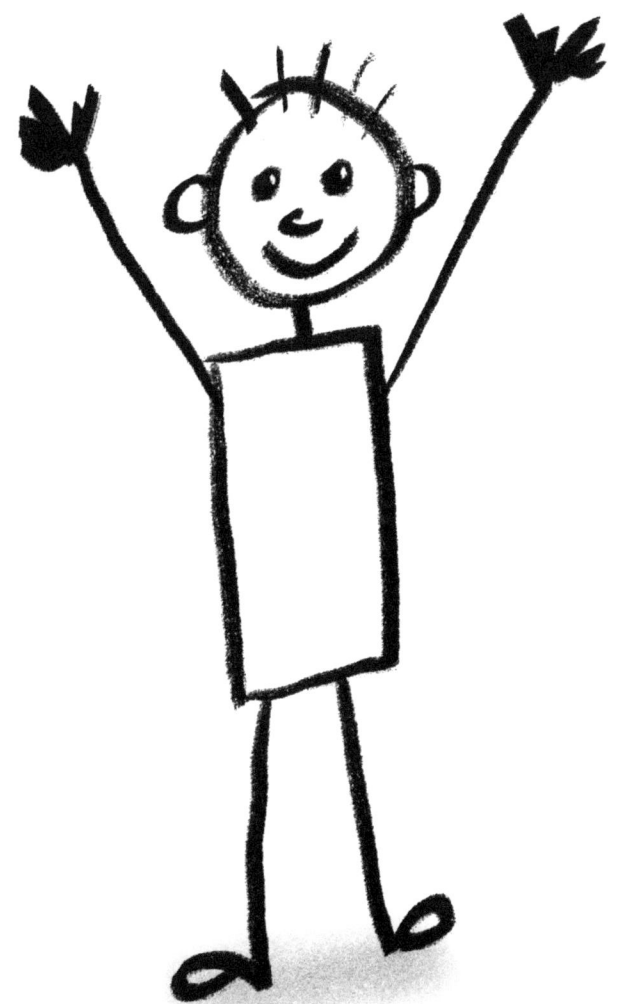

Flop!

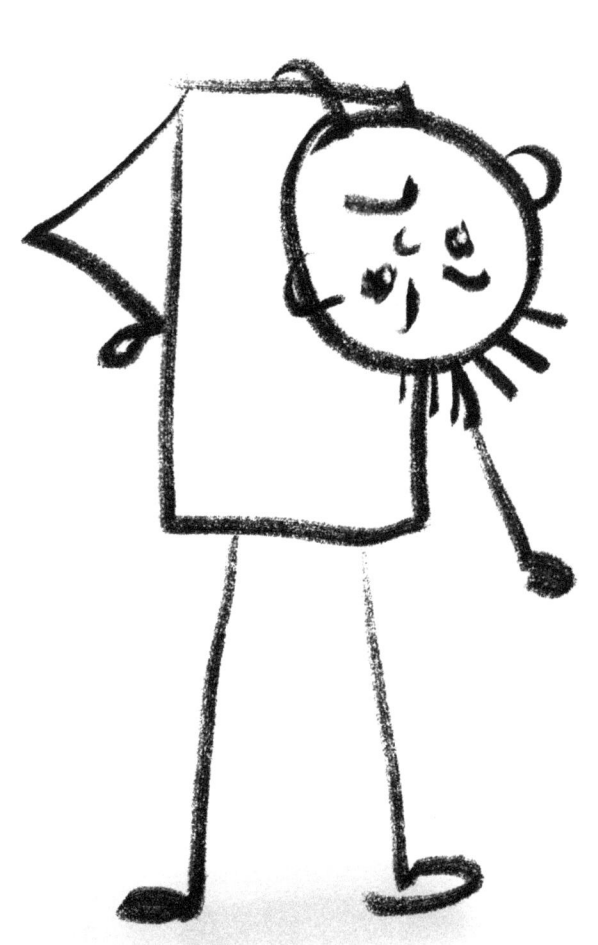

Saul grabbed his pencil again.

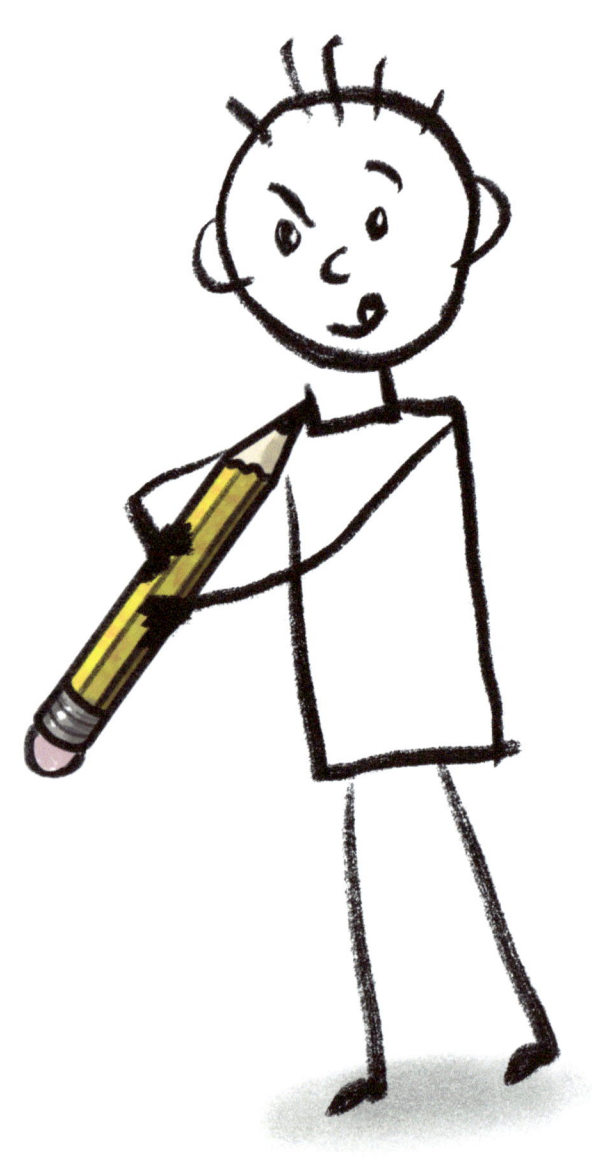

A neck!

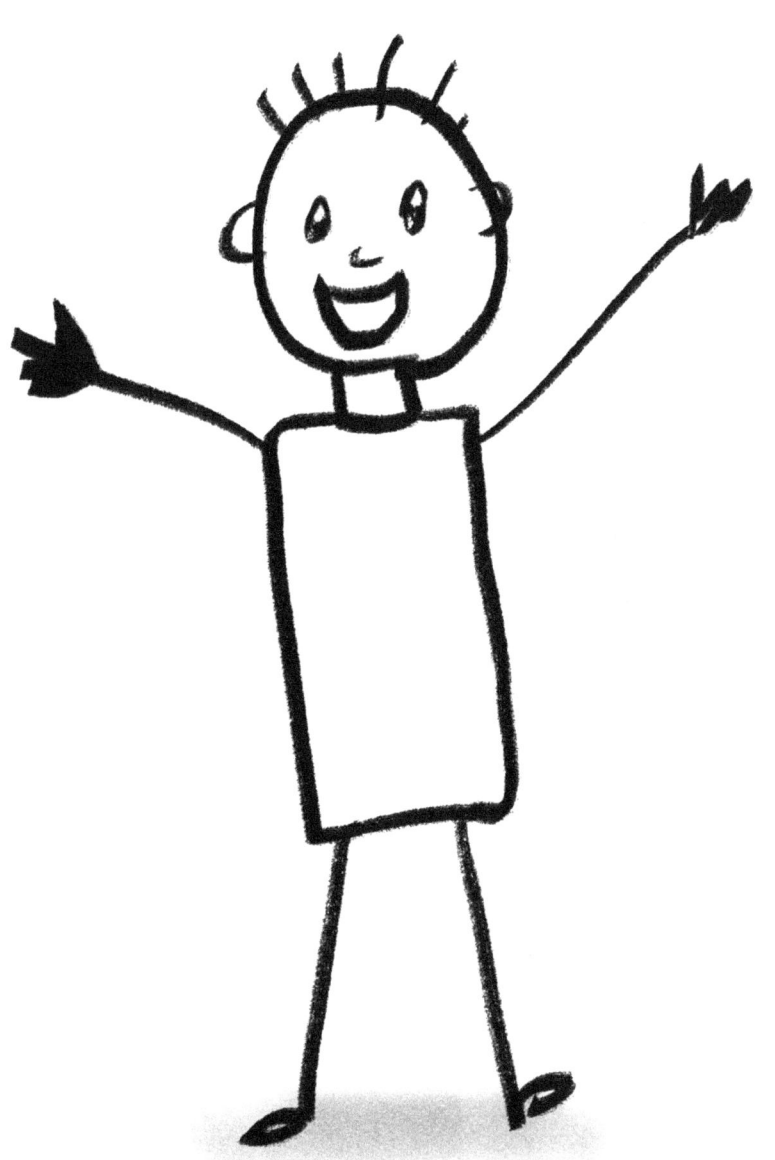

His legs began to shake.

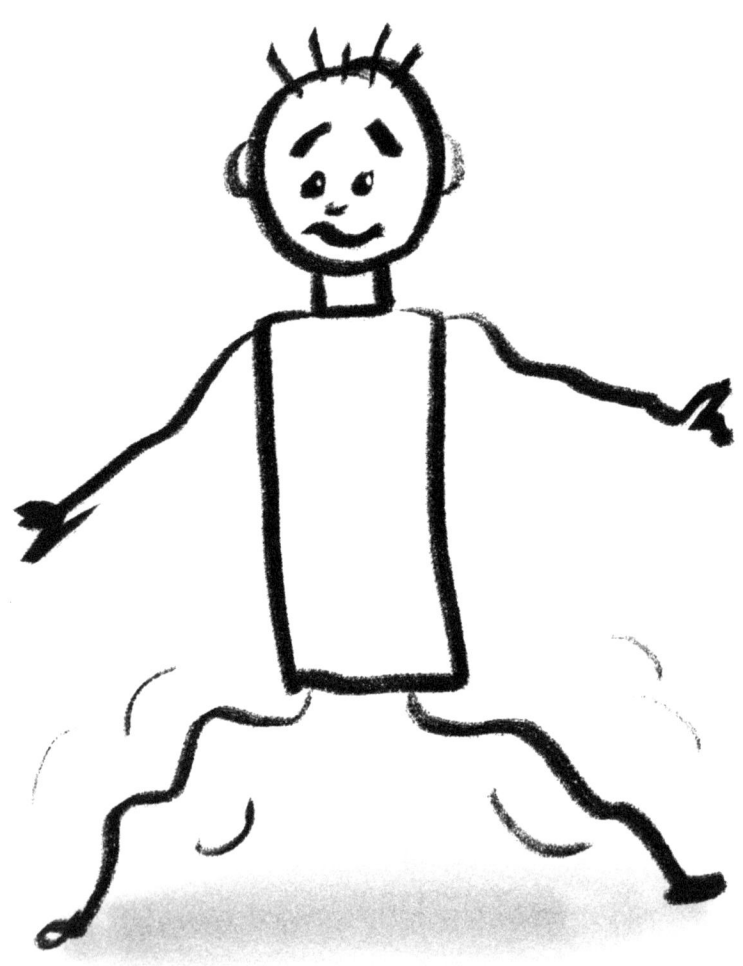

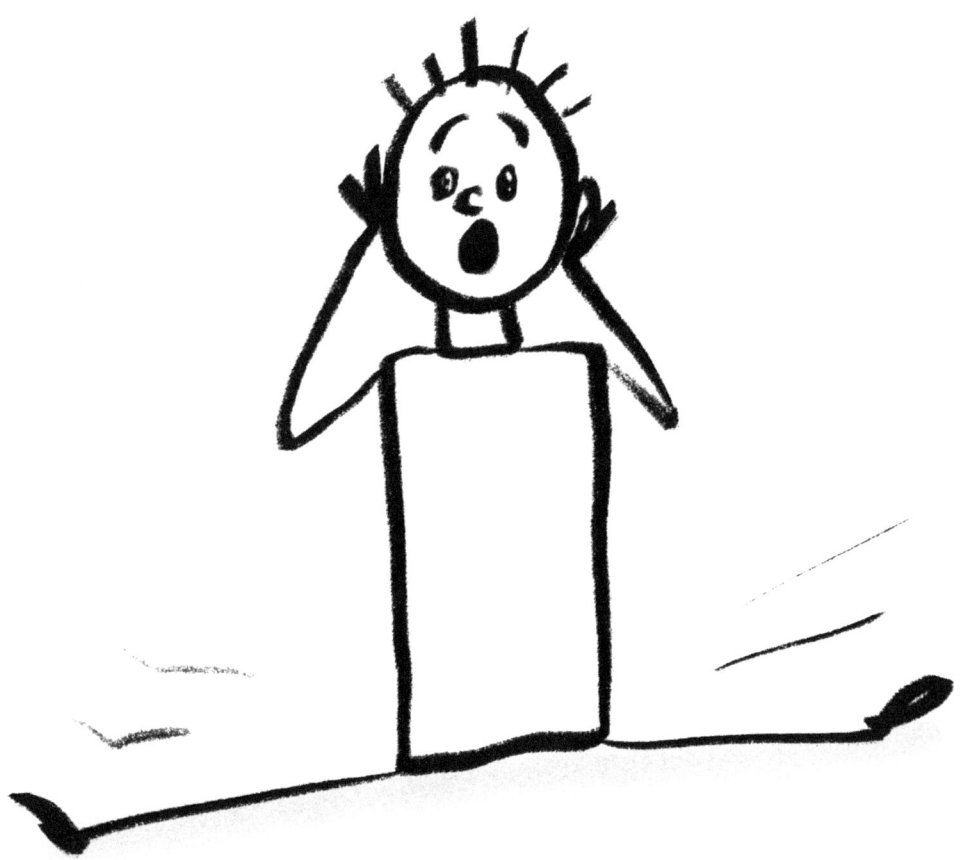

He needed legs...

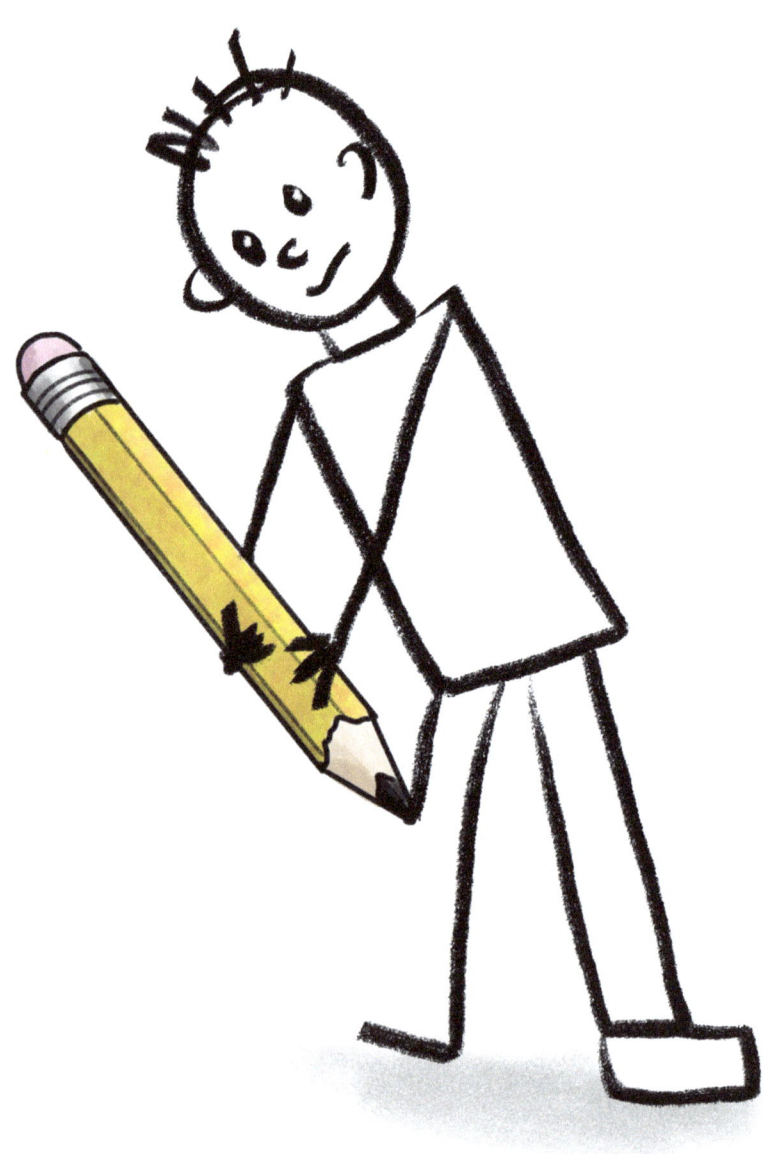

and arms!!

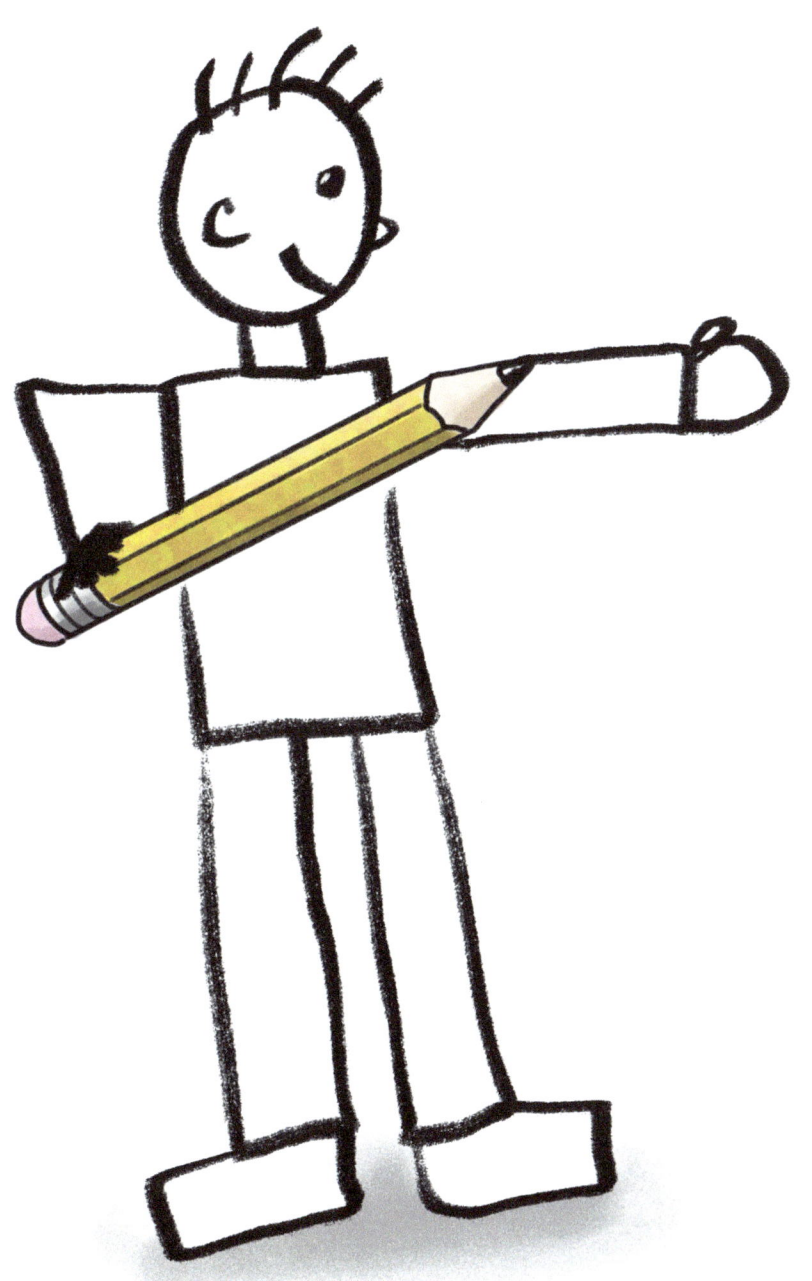

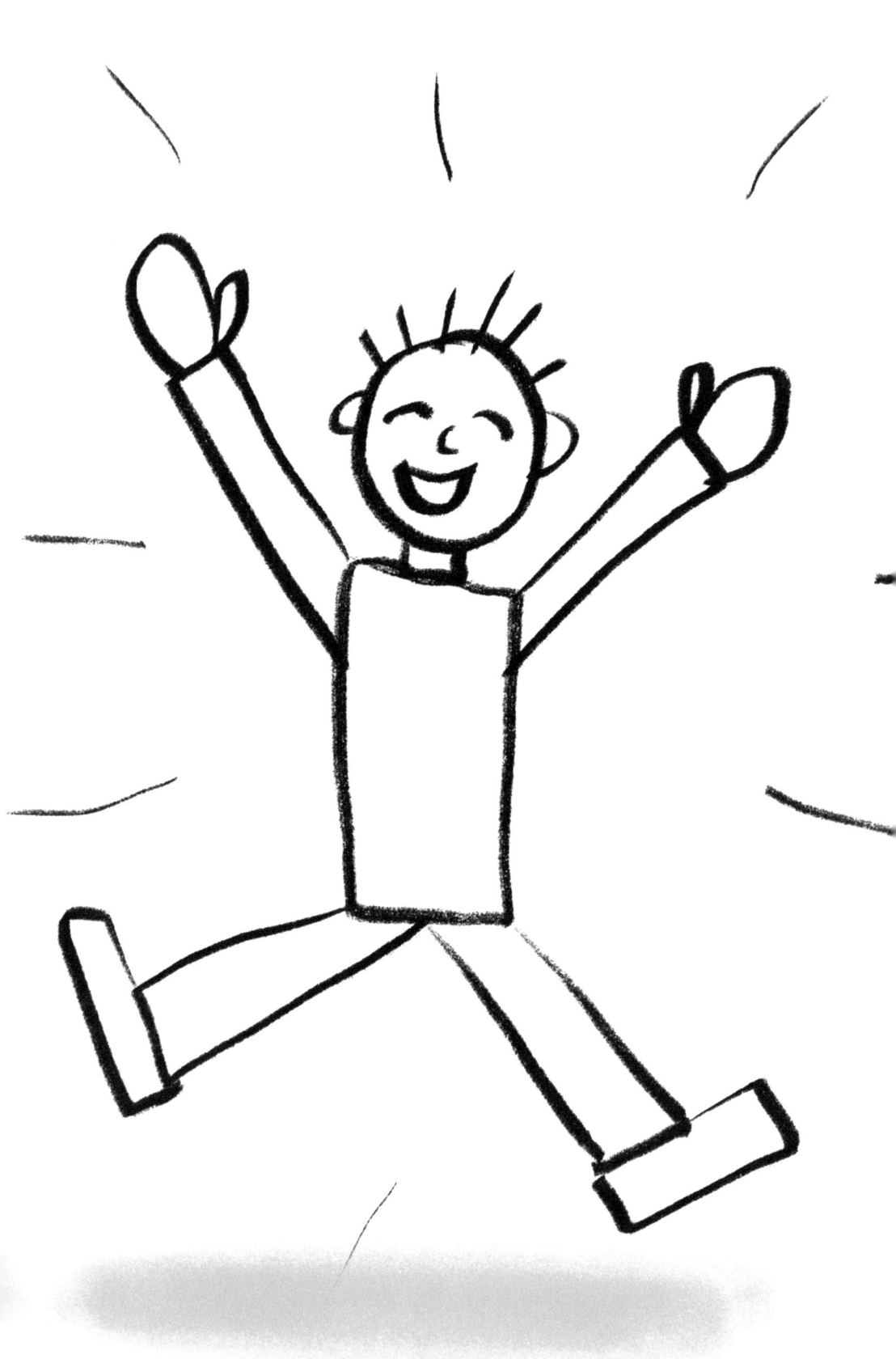

Hooray!! Now, Saul was feeling strong and steady.

He tried to do a happy dance...

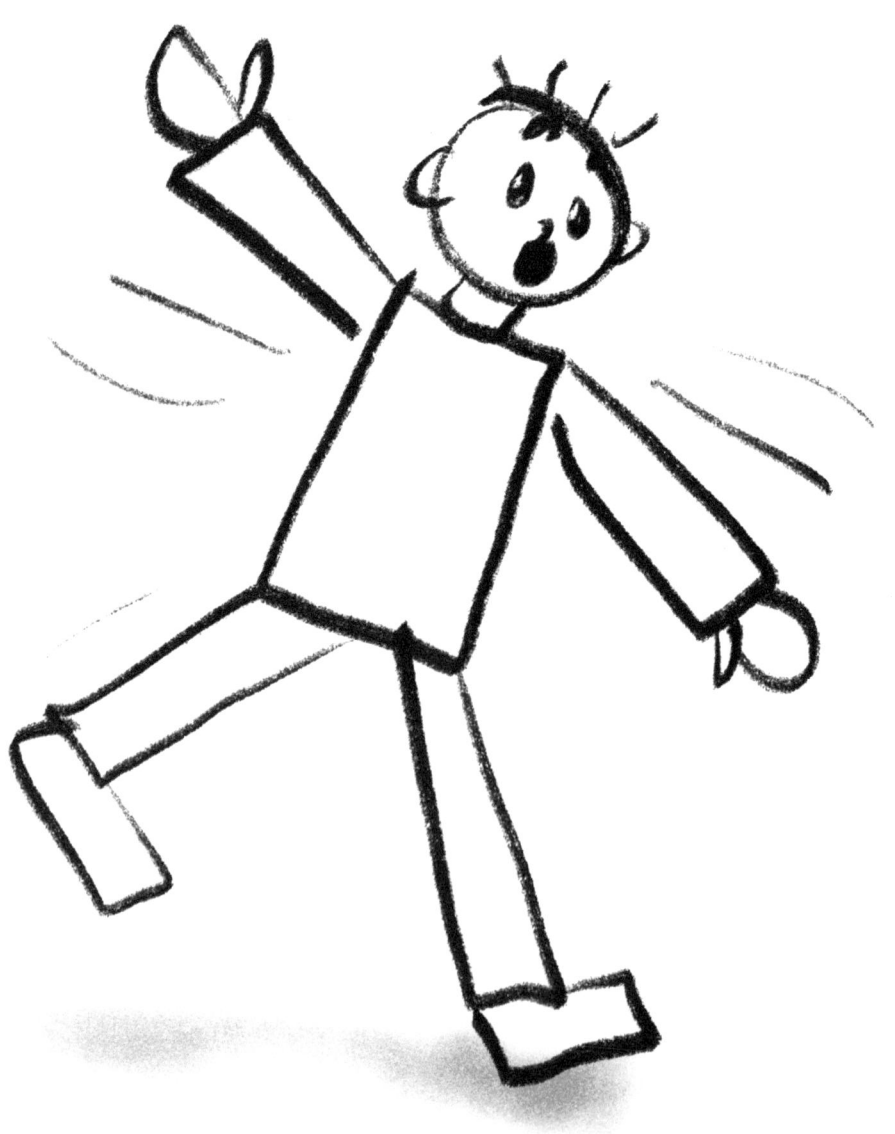

but fell on his face.

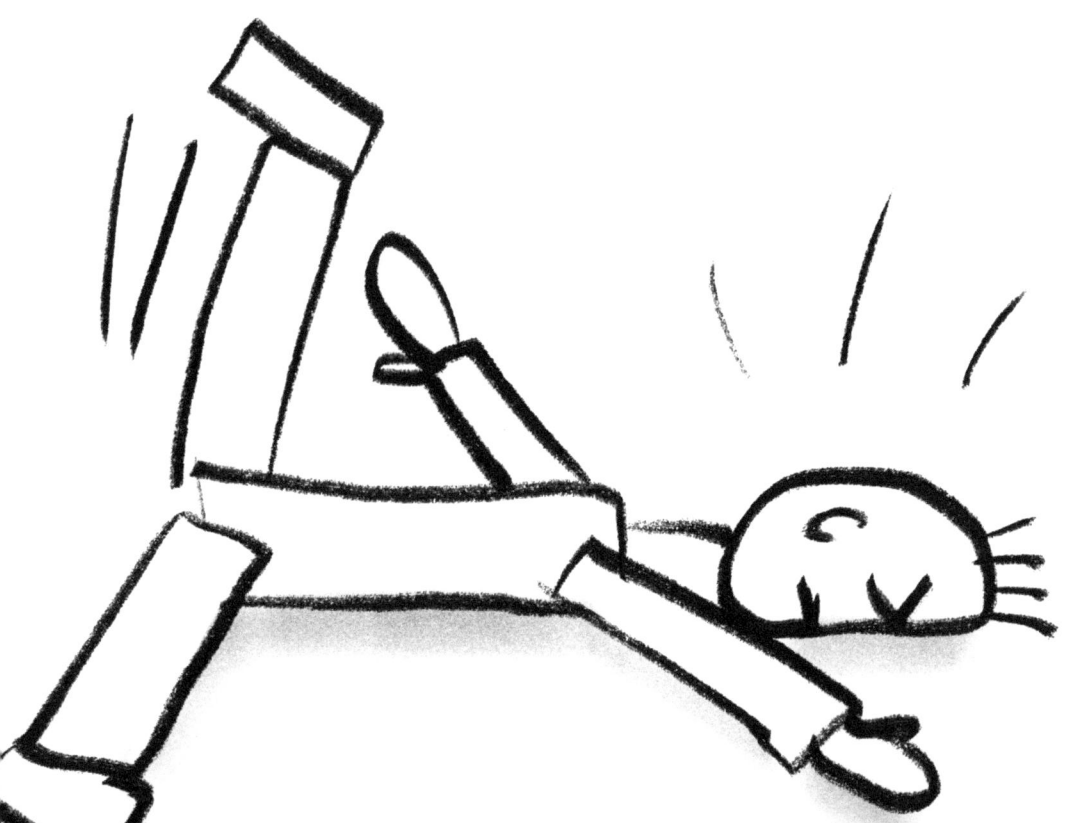

Hmmm how can I get my arms and legs to bend? Saul thought to himself.

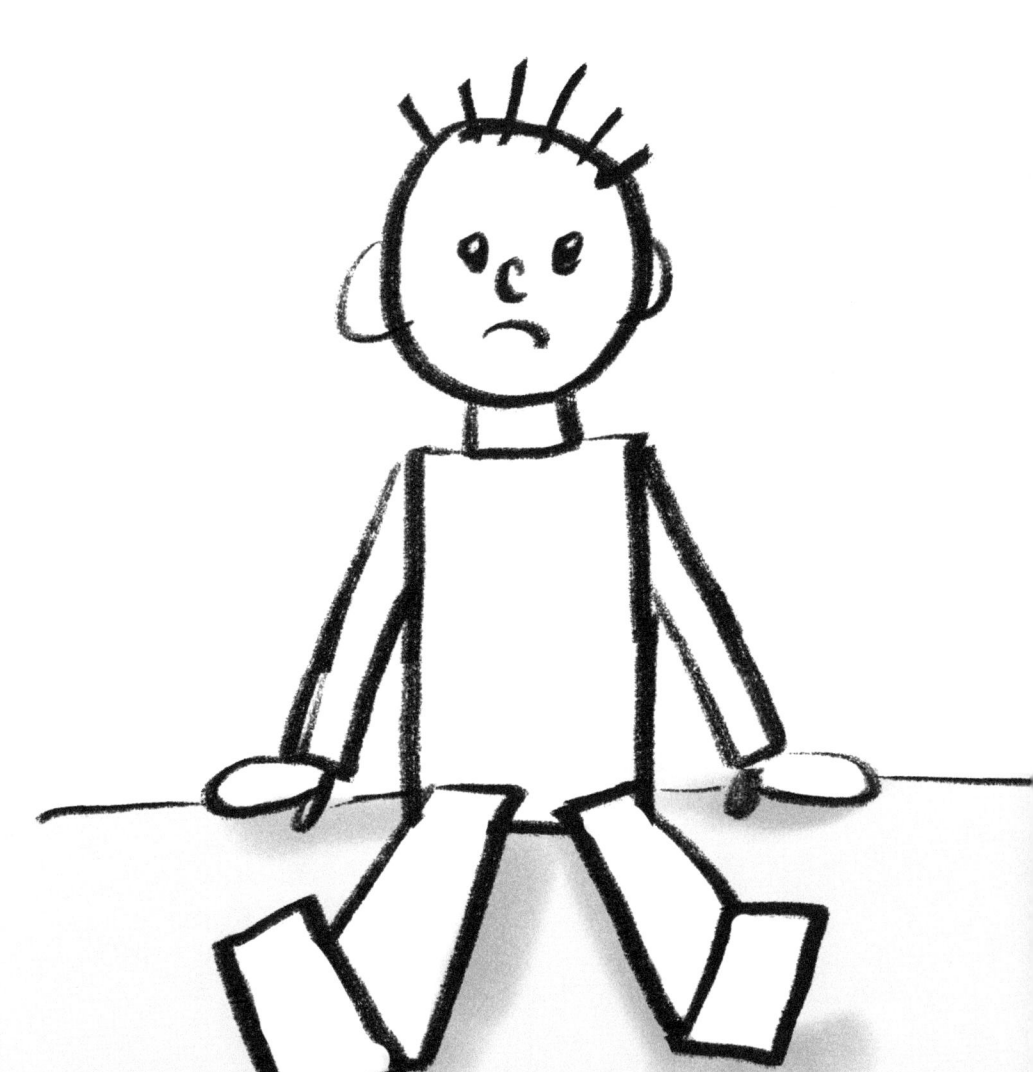

Then he got another great idea.

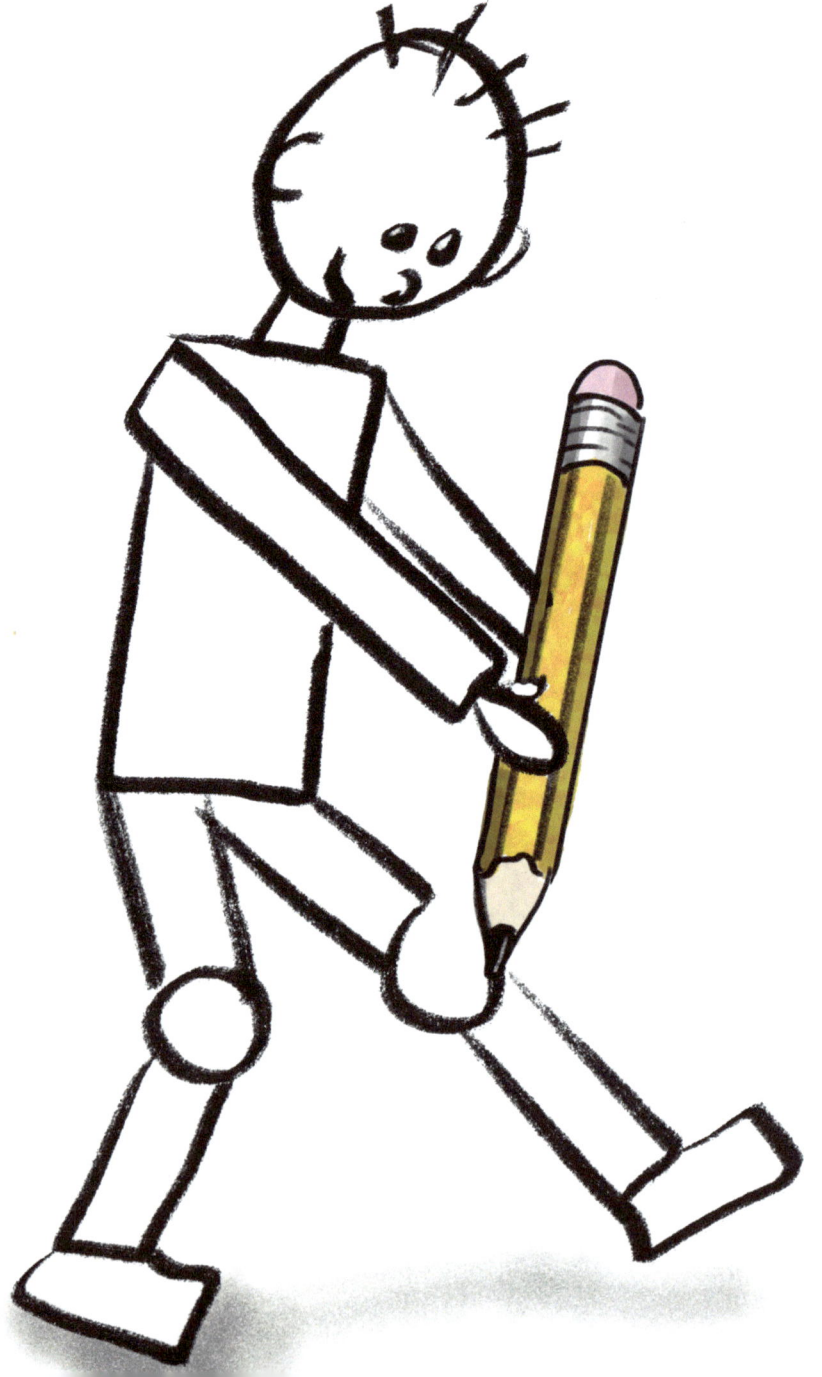

In the middle of each arm and leg, he drew a circle to help him bend.

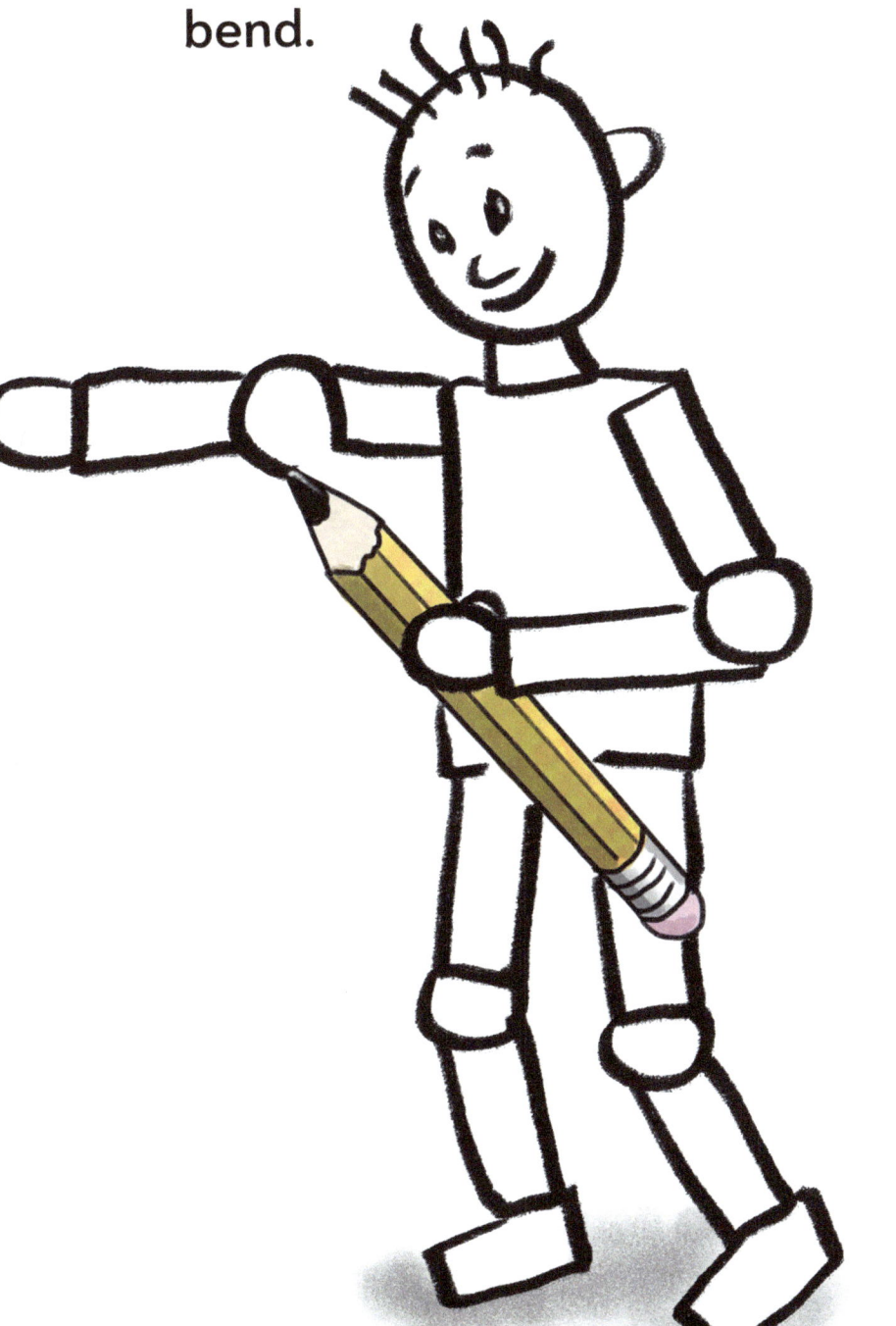

This time, he was able to do his happy dance without falling.

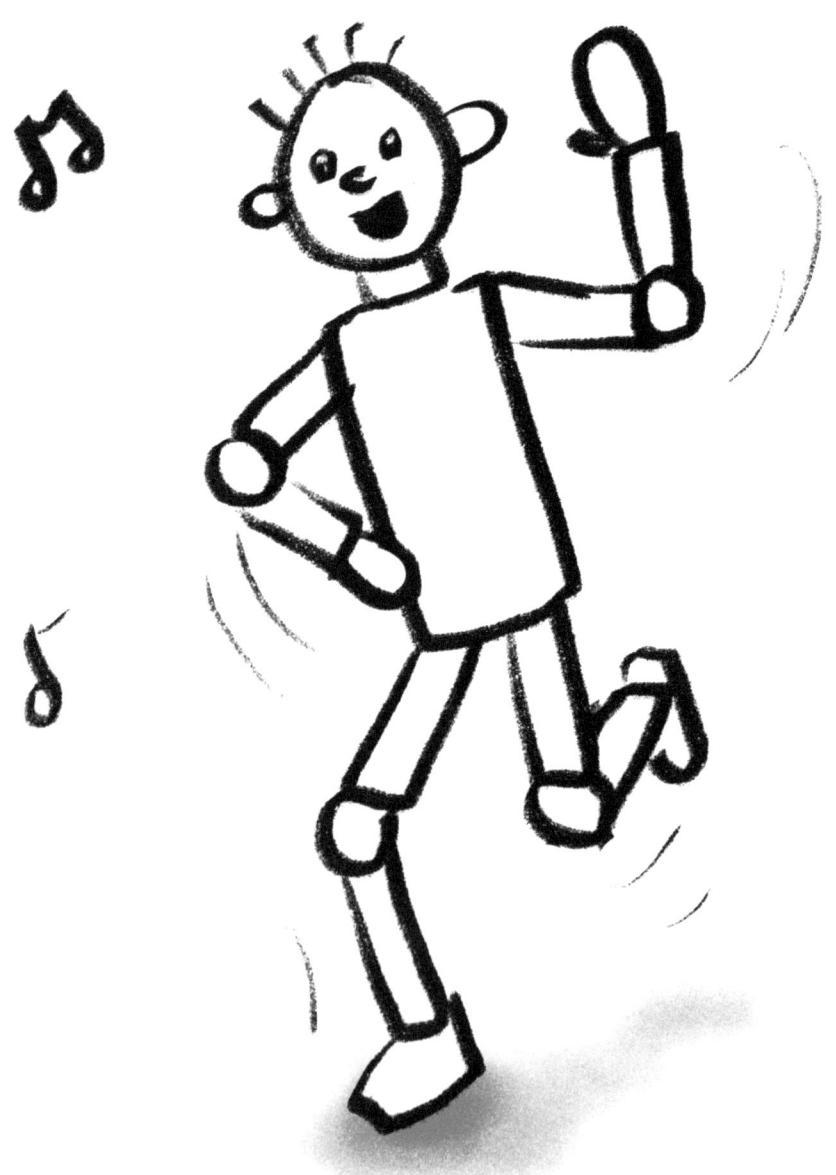

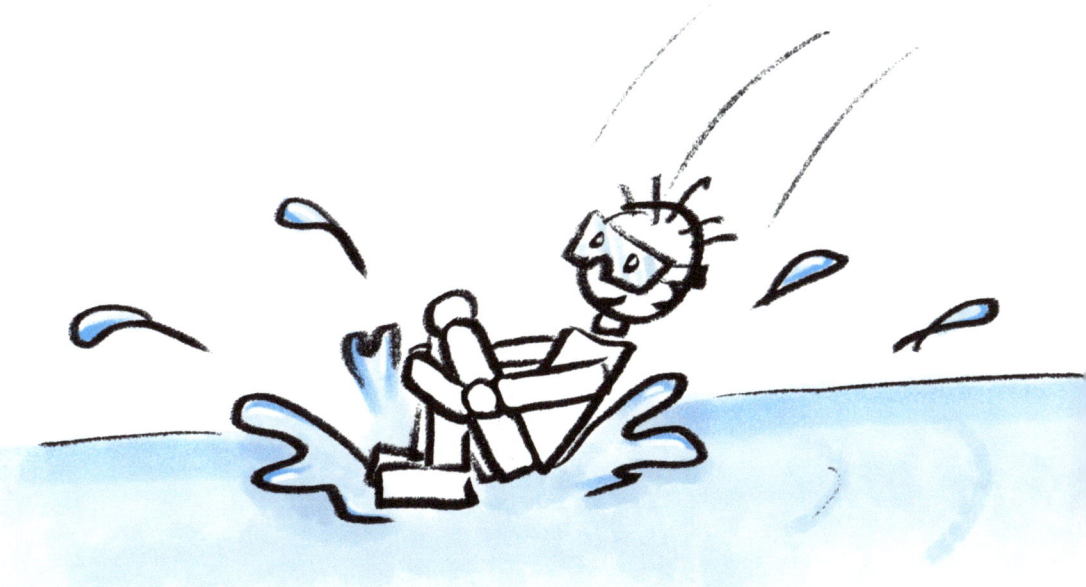

And he had no trouble doing everything else he loved.

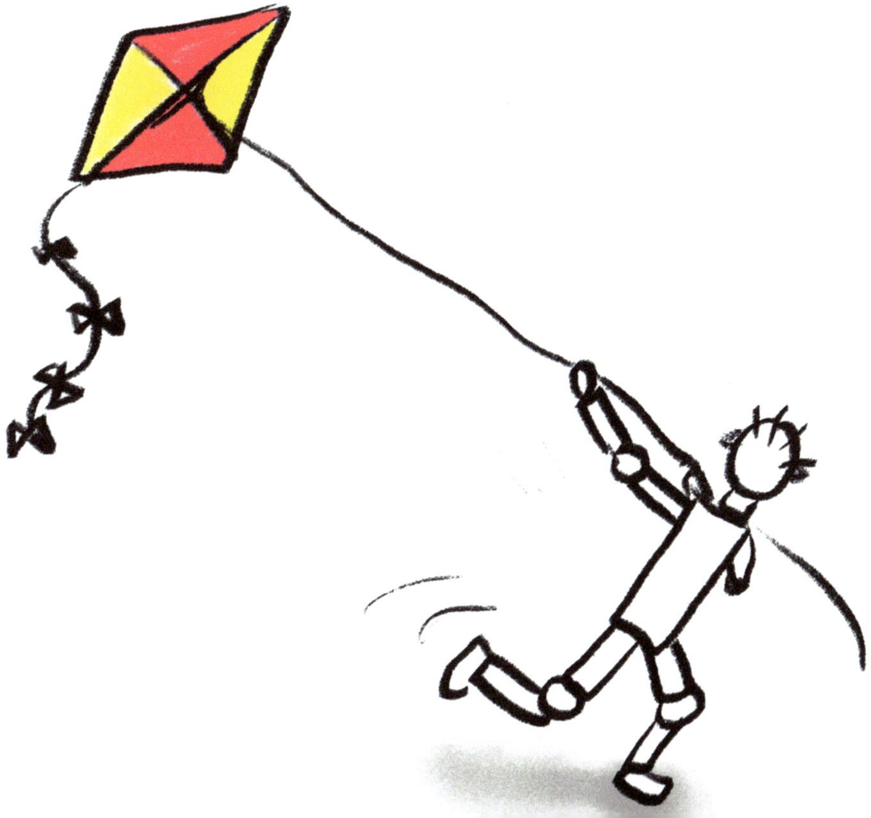

In the end, Saul the stick man wasn't a stick man anymore. He had become a very happy shape man.

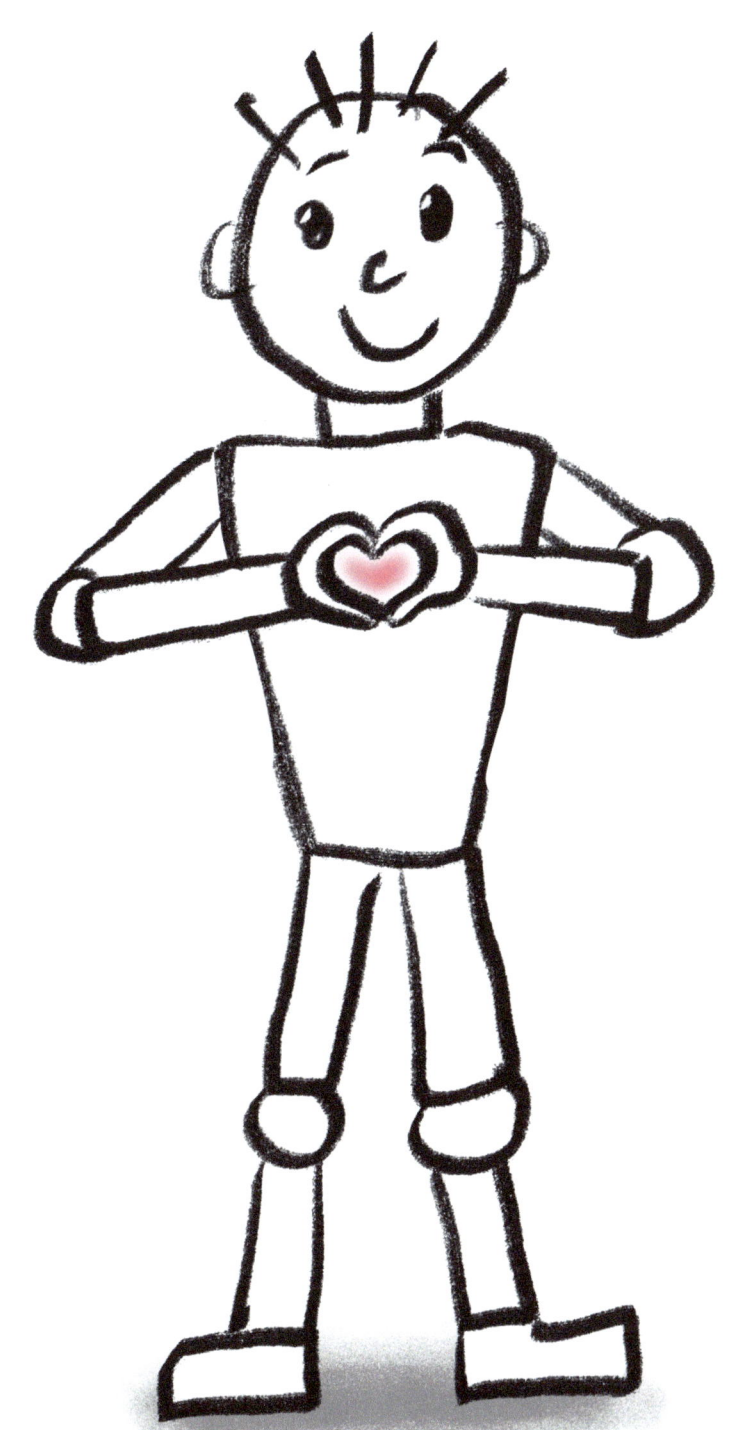

www.ingramcontent.com/pod-product-compliance
Lightning Source LLC
Chambersburg PA
CBHW040300220526
45473CB00002B/544